Unifix Phonics Blends

Using Unifix® Letter Cubes

Emily Larson-Rutter • Shelley Lapp

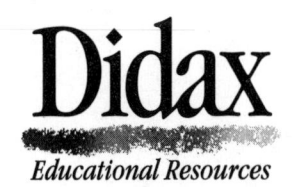

Didax
Educational Resources

Copyright © 2003 by Didax Educational Resources, Inc., Rowley, MA 01969. All rights reserved.

This book is published by Didax Educational Resources, Inc., Rowley, Massachusetts.

The publisher grants permission to the purchaser of this book to reproduce any of the blackline masters in quantities sufficient for that purchaser's classroom.

No part of this publication may be reproduced, stored in a retrieval system, or transmitted in any form or by any means – electronic, mechanical, recording, or otherwise – without the prior written permission of the publisher.

Printed in the United States of America.

Order Number 2-160
ISBN 1-58324-161-2

A B C D E F 07 06 05 04 03

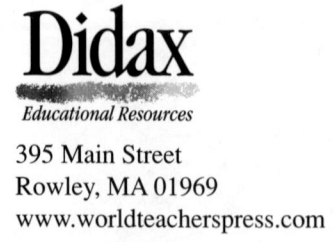

Didax
Educational Resources

395 Main Street
Rowley, MA 01969
www.worldteacherspress.com

Contents

Introduction 5
Teacher's Notes 5-6
Unit One: Beginning Blends
    Activity 1: Practice Word Practice 9
    Activity 2: New Word Challenge 9
    Activity 3: Alphabetizing Practice 10
    Activity 4: Blend Book Search 10
    Activity 5: Complete the Cloze 11
    Activity 6: Make Your Own Cloze 11
    Activity 7: Dictionary Practice 12
    Activity 8: Hangman 12
    Week 1 Blends: ch, sh, th, wh 13
    Week 2 Blends: br, cr, dr 13
    Week 3 Blends: fr, gr, pr, tr 14
    Week 4 Blends: bl, cl, fl 14
    Week 5 Blends: gl, sl 15
    Week 6 Blends: sc, sk, sm 15
    Week 7 Blends: sn, sp, st, sw 16
    Week 8 Blends: tw, wr 16
    Reproducible pages 17-25
    Word Lists 26
Unit Two: Vowel Combinations
    Activity 1: Practice Word Practice 29
    Activity 2: Word Families 29
    Activity 3: Create-a-Sentence 30
    Activity 4: Word Webs 30
    Activity 5: Alphabetizing Practice 31
    Activity 6: Synonyms 31
    Activity 7: Antonyms 32
    Activity 8: Homonyms 32
    Week 1 Vowel Combinations: ai, ay, ea, ee 33
    Week 2 Vowel Combinations: ie, oa, ue 33
    Week 3 Vowel Combinations: ar, er, ir 34
    Week 4 Vowel Combinations: or, ur 34
    Week 5 Vowel Combinations: aw, ew 35
    Week 6 Vowel Combinations: oi, oy 35
    Week 7 Vowel Combinations: ou, ow 36
    Week 8 Vowel Combinations: ea, oo, ow 36
    Reproducible pages 37-39
    Word Lists 40

Contents

Unit Three: Final Blends
- Activity 1: Practice Word Practice — **43**
- Activity 2: New Word Challenge — **43**
- Activity 3: Build-A-Word — **44**
- Activity 4: Cube Draw — **44**
- Activity 5: Word Unscramble — **45**
- Activity 6: Crossword Puzzle — **45**
- Activity 7: Build the Answer — **46**
- Activity 8: Partner Pass — **46**
- Week 1 Final Blends: ch, ck, sh, th — **47**
- Week 2 Final Blends: sk, ss, st — **47**
- Week 3 Final Blends: ld, lf, lk, ll, lt — **48**
- Week 4 Final Blends: ff, ft — **48**
- Week 5 Final Blends: nd, nt — **49**
- Week 6 Final Blends: mp — **49**
- Week 7 Final Blends: ng, nk — **50**
- Week 8 Final Blends: gh, gn, lk — **50**
- Word Lists — **51**

Appendix A
- Synonyms/Antonyms/Homonyms Word Lists **52**

Appendix B
- Blend Clip Art — **53-56**

Introduction

In our classrooms, we have found that many students learn best in a "hands-on" learning situation. Typically, spelling and phonics instruction has been an auditory and visual activity followed up by pencil and paper worksheets. Unifix Letter Cubes provide an avenue for teaching spelling/phonics patterns in a way that gives auditory, visual and kinesthetic cues. As students are allowed to hear, see and then do, a deeper level of understanding can be achieved. Using the cubes is a fun and interesting way for students to learn new concepts or practice those already introduced.

Teacher's Notes

Student Group Configuration
This book is intended for small group instruction of up to eight students. You will have contact with each student several times during a short lesson. You can group students according to ability so that all students in your group are working on the same concept or skill. Alternatively, students can be mixed in ability and working on different skills as you monitor. Lessons are intended to be brief – perhaps 15 to 20 minutes in length.

How to Use this Activity Book
This book is divided into three units: Initial Blends, Vowel Combinations and Final Blends. Each unit begins with activities for teaching the blends in that unit. Most of these activities and games are general in nature and can be applied to any or all of the blends in that unit. The activities are presented in a logical order for teaching. That is, introductory activities are presented first followed by more difficult lesson ideas. Reproducible worksheets are included for several activities.

Example Activity Page

Introduction 5

Teacher's Notes

Eight instructional weeks of blends follow the activities. Each week you will be teaching a set of blends that are similar in structure, follow the same phonetic rule, or make similar sounds. When you begin a new week, please begin with Activity One. This activity introduces the blends being covered that week and the Practice Words that are used in later activities. After Activity One, choose any activities you like.

On the blend pages, space is provided for you to list other words you and your students particularly like or find helpful.

Please remember that the ideas in this book are only a starting point for you. You will most likely create many more activities specific to the needs of your students. Remember to jot them down in the spaces provided so they will be at your fingertips the next time you need them!

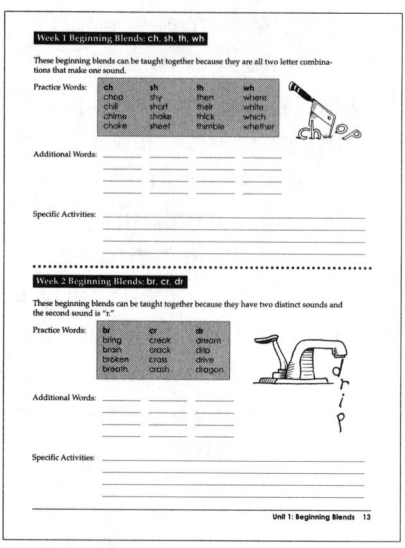

Example Blends Page

A Word List appears at the end of each unit. The words are listed in the order the blends are taught. Use these lists as a handy reference when thinking of examples for students.

Blend Clip Art finishes up the book. Most of the blends are covered by a couple of pieces of artwork. This artwork can be used for flashcards, mini posters, coloring sheets, or anything else you can think up.

Unit One: Beginning Blends

Activity 1: Practice Word Practice

Materials: Unifix Blend Cubes
Unifix Consonant and Vowel Cubes

Instructions: Write the blend for the day in large letters where all students in the group can see it. Have students build the provided Practice Words one by one. Discuss pronunciations of the blend and the words. Post the provided Practice Words prominently in the classroom for referral all week with other activities.

Activity 2: New Word Challenge

Materials: Unifix Blend Cubes
Unifix Consonant and Vowel Cubes

Instructions: Write the blend for the day in large letters where all students can see it. Have students use the cubes to create a word beginning with the blend that they think no one else will get. Reveal the words one by one. You can even give points to students who create a word no one else created. Start over.

Unit 1: Beginning Blends 9

Activity 3: Alphabetizing Practice

Materials: Alphabetizing Practice Worksheet, page 25

Instructions: Pass out an Alphabetizing Practice Worksheet to each student. Have children alphabetize the words created in Activity 2.

Activity 4: Blend Book Search

Materials: Unifix Blend Cubes
Unifix Consonant and Vowel Cubes
Reading Textbooks
Chart Paper and Marker

Instructions: Open reading textbooks to a common page. Have students scan the page for the blend and build the words they find with their cubes. For extra reinforcement, record these words on chart paper to display in the classroom.

Activity 5: Complete the Cloze

Materials: Unifix Blend Cubes
Unifix Consonant and Vowel Cubes
Cloze Sentence Strips

Preparation: Photocopy the Cloze Sentence Strips for the appropriate week's blends, enlarging 200% so that cubes will fit in the spaces. Make one set of strips for each group of students. Strips can be laminated for durability.

Instructions: Pass out sentence strips and cubes to student groups. Have students make a word out of their cubes to complete a selected sentence, fitting the cubes on the strip. After you check their response, the strip can be passed to the next student in the group or put back in a common pile. Play a game by having students complete as many strips as possible in a set time.

Activity 6: Make Your Own Cloze

Materials: Unifix Blend Cubes
Unifix Consonant and Vowel Cubes
Blank Paper

Instructions: After they are proficient with Activity 5, have students create cloze sentences of their own. Have students exchange and solve the sentences.

Unit 1: Beginning Blends

Activity 7: Dictionary Practice

Materials: Unifix Blend Cubes
Unifix Consonant and Vowel Cubes
Student Dictionaries

Instructions: Have students build the Practice Words one at a time and then look them up in the dictionary. Students should already have an understanding of guide words for this activity.

Activity 8: Letter Cube Hangman

Materials: Unifix Blend Cubes
Unifix Consonant and Vowel Cubes
Blank Paper

Instructions: Students take turns being the leader of the game. Have the leader choose and build a Practice Word, keeping the word hidden. As in traditional Hangman, students take turns guessing letters. As the players guess correctly, the leader must give away his or her letter cubes. Whoever has the most cubes at the end of the game wins.

12 Unifix Phonics Blends

Week 1 Beginning Blends: ch, sh, th, wh

These beginning blends can be taught together because they are all two letter combinations that make one sound.

Practice Words:

ch	sh	th	wh
chop	shy	then	where
chill	short	their	white
chime	shake	thick	which
choke	sheet	thimble	whether

Additional Words: _____

Specific Activities: _____

- - -

Week 2 Beginning Blends: br, cr, dr

These beginning blends can be taught together because they have two distinct sounds and the second sound is "r."

Practice Words:

br	cr	dr
bring	creak	dream
brain	crack	drip
broken	cross	drive
breath	crash	dragon

Additional Words: _____

Specific Activities: _____

Unit 1: Beginning Blends

Week 3 Beginning Blends: fr, gr, pr, tr

These beginning blends are a continuation of the blends from Week 2 and can be taught together because they contain two distinct sounds. The second sound is "r."

Practice Words:

fr	gr	pr	tr
friend	growth	prance	tribe
freedom	grumpy	print	track
frighten	grind	praise	treat
freeze	grand	prize	trout

Additional Words: _____

Specific Activities: _____

Week 4 Beginning Blends: bl, cl, fl

These beginning blends can be taught together because they have two distinct sounds and the second sound is "l."

Practice Words:

bl	cl	fl
blend	clean	flower
black	clock	flame
bleed	claim	flight
blame	climb	flag

Additional Words: _____

Specific Activities: _____

14   Unifix Phonics Blends

Week 5 Beginning Blends: gl, sl

These beginning blends are a continuation of the blends from Week 4 in which the blends have two distinct sounds and the second sound is "l."

Practice Words:

gl	sl
glove	slither
glamour	slave
glide	slink
glitter	sloppy

Additional Words: _____ _____
_____ _____
_____ _____
_____ _____

Specific Activities: _____
_____
_____
_____

• •

Week 6 Beginning Blends: sc, sk, sm

These beginning blends can be taught together because they have two distinct sounds, the first being "s."

Practice Words:

sc	sk	sm
scare	skip	smile
scamper	sky	smoke
scorch	skill	smell
scramble	skim	smart

Additional Words: _____ _____ _____
_____ _____ _____
_____ _____ _____
_____ _____ _____

Specific Activities: _____
_____
_____
_____

Unit 1: Beginning Blends

Week 7 Beginning Blends: sn, sp, st, sw

These beginning blends can be taught together because they all contain two distinct sounds, the first being "s."

Practice Words:

sn	sp	st	sw
snack	spell	stamp	sweet
snail	sports	steam	swell
sniffle	sparkle	sticky	swamp
sneeze	spade	stagger	swift

Additional Words: _____ _____ _____ _____

Specific Activities: _____

Week 8 Beginning Blends: tw, wr

These beginning blends can be taught together because they both are unusual blends.

Practice Words:

tw	wr
twist	wrestle
twine	wrist
tweet	wrinkle
twinkle	wraps

Additional Words: _____ _____

Specific Activities: _____

16   Unifix Phonics Blends

Complete the Cloze Sentence Strips: Week 1

Instructions: Enlarge strips 200% to allow cubes to fit properly.

After you cut down the tree, ☐☐☐ it up for firewood.
Hint: ch

It is fun to ☐☐☐ with your friends on the telephone.
Hint: ch

☐☐☐ the door behind you when you go outside.
Hint: sh

What is your favorite television ☐☐☐?
Hint: sh

Saying ☐☐☐☐ ☐☐☐ is polite.
Hint: th

Father put the frozen cake on the table to ☐☐☐.
Hint: th

☐☐☐ time is it?
Hint: wh

My brother couldn't remember ☐☐☐☐ he put the soccer ball.
Hint: wh

Answers: chop, chat, shut, show, thank you, thaw, what, where

Unit 1: Beginning Blends 17

Complete the Cloze Sentence Strips: Week 2

Instructions: Enlarge strips 200% to allow cubes to fit properly.

Always remember to ☐☐☐☐ your pencils to school.
Hint: br

Aunt Sue put the ☐☐☐☐ in the toaster.
Hint: br

Babies sometimes ☐☐.
Hint: cr

There was a ☐☐☐☐ when Arnie dropped the plates.
Hint: cr

Marcy ☐☐☐☐ all her milk at once.
Hint: dr

Mom used a hammer and ☐☐☐☐ to fix the cupboard.
Hint: dr

Answers: bring, bread, cry, crash, drank, drill

18 Unifix Phonics Blends

Complete the Cloze Sentence Strips: Week 3

Instructions: Enlarge strips 200% to allow cubes to fit properly.

The ice cubes melted because they were not in the ☐☐☐☐☐☐. Hint: fr

It is fun to play with my best ☐☐☐☐☐. Hint: fr

The traffic light is ☐☐☐☐☐ so we can go. Hint: gr

One of Freddie's chores is to mow the ☐☐☐☐☐. Hint: gr

In first grade, we learned to ☐☐☐☐☐ our names. Hint: pr

Ronald came in first in the race and won the ☐☐☐☐☐. Hint: pr

Suzanne climbed the ☐☐☐☐ to see in the upstairs window. Hint: tr

Mary's father drove the big ☐☐☐☐☐ into the garage. Hint: tr

Answers: freezer, friend, green, grass, print, prize, tree, truck

Unit 1: Beginning Blends   19

Complete the Cloze Sentence Strips: Week 4

Instructions: Enlarge strips 200% to allow cubes to fit properly.

The baby loves to stack up her ☐☐☐☐☐.

Hint: bl

Carrie's eyes are as ☐☐☐ as the sky.

Hint: bl

The cat has very sharp ☐☐☐☐.

Hint: cl

Doug kept all his clothes in the ☐☐☐☐☐.

Hint: cl

Sweep the dirt up off the ☐☐☐☐.

Hint: fl

The dog was scratching because of his ☐☐☐☐.

Hint: fl

Answers: blocks, blue, claws, closet, floor, fleas

20 Unifix Phonics Blends

Complete the Cloze Sentence Strips: Week 5

Instructions: Enlarge strips 200% to allow cubes to fit properly.

The beautiful ☐☐☐☐ vase was filled with flowers. Hint: gl

Fireflies ☐☐☐ in the dark. Hint: gl

I lost my ☐☐☐☐ while I was playing in the snow. Hint: gl

The baseball player ☐☐☐ into home plate. Hint: sl

Don't ☐☐☐☐ the door. Hint: sl

The kids were watching the snake ☐☐☐☐☐☐☐ through the yard. Hint: sl

Answers: glass, glow, glove, slid, slam, slither

Unit 1: Beginning Blends

Complete the Cloze Sentence Strips: Week 6

Instructions: Enlarge strips 200% to allow cubes to fit properly.

Ashley was wearing red mittens and a red ☐☐☐☐.
Hint: sc

The little boy fell and ☐☐☐☐☐☐ his knee.
Hint: sc

The dark clouds rolled across the ☐☐.
Hint: sk

A ☐☐☐☐ is a black animal with a white stripe.
Hint: sk

The campfire was making black ☐☐☐☐.
Hint: sm

The photographer asked me to ☐☐☐☐ for my picture.
Hint: sm

Answers: scarf, scraped, sky, skunk, smoke, smile

22 Unifix Phonics Blends

Complete the Cloze Sentence Strips: Week 7

Instructions: Enlarge strips 200% to allow cubes to fit properly.

The ☐☐☐ slithered along in the grass.
Hint: sn

Can you ☐☐☐ your fingers?
Hint: sn

Use the dictionary if you don't know how to ☐☐☐☐ a word.
Hint: sp

The astronaut went up into ☐☐☐☐.
Hint: sp

Aunt Sally forgot to put a ☐☐☐☐ on the letter.
Hint: st

When the traffic light is red, we need to ☐☐☐.
Hint: st

You can use the broom to ☐☐☐☐ the floor.
Hint: sw

The candy was ☐☐☐.
Hint: sw

Answers: snake, snap, spell, space, stamp, stop, sweep, sweet

Unit 1: Beginning Blends 23

Complete the Cloze Sentence Strips: Week 8

Instructions: Enlarge strips 200% to allow cubes to fit properly.

The ☐☐☐☐ are identical.

Hint: tw

Stars ☐☐☐☐☐☐ in the night sky.

Hint: tw

I like to listen to the birds ☐☐☐☐ in the springtime.

Hint: tw

James got only one question ☐☐☐☐ on the test.

Hint: wr

☐☐☐☐ the water from the washcloth.

Hint: wr

Dad ironed the ☐☐☐☐☐☐ out of my favorite pants.

Hint: wr

Answers: twins, twinkle, tweet, wrong, wring, wrinkle

24 Unifix Phonics Blends

Alphabetizing Practice

Name: _____

a b c d e f g h i j k l m n o p q r s t u v w x y z

1. _____
2. _____
3. _____
4. _____
5. _____
6. _____
7. _____
8. _____
9. _____
10. _____
11. _____
12. _____
13. _____
14. _____
15. _____
16. _____

- -

Alphabetizing Practice

Name: _____

a b c d e f g h i j k l m n o p q r s t u v w x y z

1. _____
2. _____
3. _____
4. _____
5. _____
6. _____
7. _____
8. _____
9. _____
10. _____
11. _____
12. _____
13. _____
14. _____
15. _____
16. _____

Word Lists: Beginning Blends

ch
chat
children
chief
church
chart
change
chin
chance
chest
cheer
chain
check
chase

sh
she
shall
show
ship
short
shape
shot
shirt
shell
sheet
shop
shut

th
thank
think
thing
third
thirty
thick
thought
thread
threw
thumb
thunder
threat

wh
when
what
which
whether
where
white
while
why
wheat
whale
whip
whisper

whistle
wheeze
wharf
whack
whiff
whimper
whiz

br
bread
break
brick
broad
brother
brown
bring
breath
branch
bright
broken
brave
brush
breeze
bridge
brain
brass
breakfast

cr
cry
crack
crowd
crash
cream
crew
crazy
cross
crow
create
cried
crops
crayon
creek
crown
cruel
credit

dr
dry
draw
drug
drove
drop
dress
dream
dragon

drill
drink
drive
drew
drift
drama
drain
drip
drench
droop

fr
free
from
front
friend
Friday
fry
frost
frank
freshman
frame
fresh
fraction
fruit
freedom
frozen
France
freighter
fragile
frisky

gr
grade
great
grow
grew
grass
gray
grand
green
ground
group
grab
grain
grant
grin
gradual
grandfather
gravity

pr
pretty
price
press
prize

print
president
prince
program
practice
prepare
present
problem
produce
property
provide
probably
prove
pray
products

tr
track
tractor
train
trade
truly
try
trick
travel
tree
trim
trip
true
trouble
trap
trail
triangle
traffic

bl
black
blue
bleed
blood
blind
blame
bloom
blossom
blond
blade
blank
blast
blend
blot
blink
blur
blow
blanket
bleach

cl
clean
cloth
clay
claim
club
clear
class
clap
claws
clerk
clever
cliff
close
cloud
clues
climb
click

fl
flower
flat
flight
flew
fly
float
floor
flavor
flood
flute
flame
flash
fleet
flow
flap
flock
fling
flip
flea
fluffy

gl
glad
globe
glow
glory
glove
glisten
gloom
glue
glum
glamour
glare
glass
glade
gleam

glee
glider
glimpse
glitter
glance
glaze

sl
slow
sleep
slept
slip
slid
slap
sled
slave
sleeve
slant
slice
slight
slope
slam
slate
slipper
sleet
slim
sly
slash
slab
sleek
slimy

sc
score
school
screen
scratch
scarf
scar
scatter
scholar
scout
scare
scramble
scrape
scream
scallop
screw
scared
scab
scoop
scrub

sk
sky
skin

skill
skunk
skirt
skip
skeleton
skull
skid
sketch
ski
skim
skillet
skirmish
skinny
skylark
skeptic

sm
smile
smooth
smell
smart
smother
smash
smear
smith
smolder
smack
smog
smock
smoky
smudge
smuggle
smug
smitten
smote

sn
snow
snowball
snare
sneeze
snore
snug
snuggle
snip
snarl
snap
snack
snail
snapshot
sneak
snatch
sneakers
sneer
sniff
sniffle

snipe
snob
snoop
snooze
snorkel
snort
snout
snub
snuff
snowman
sniper
snowy

sp
sports
space
speak
spring
spread
special
speed
spell
spot
spin
spoke
spare
spider
spend
spark

st
stop
step
stay
state
still
store
story
street
stand
star
study
strong
stick
stone
stood

sw
swim
swell
swept
sweat
sweater
sweep
switch
swallow

swing
swamp
sweet
swift
swan
swagger
swap
swollen
sway
swine
swoop
swirl
swat
swerve
sworn
swish
swear

tw
twelve
twenty
twice
twig
twirl
twine
tweed
twilight
twinkle
twist
twitter
twitch
twinge
twentieth
tweet
twelfth
twill

wr
write
writing
written
wrote
wrong
wrap
wrestle
wrist
wreath
wring
wreck
wren
wretch
wrinkle
wiggle
wrung
wry
wrangle

Unit Two: Vowel Combinations

Activity 1: Practice Word Practice

Materials: Unifix Blend Cubes
Unifix Consonant and Vowel Cubes

Instructions: Write the blend for the day in large letters where all students in the group can see it. Have students build the provided Practice Words one by one. Discuss pronunciations of the blend and the words. Post the provided Practice Words prominently in the classroom for referral all week with other activities.

Activity 2: Word Families

Materials: Word Families Booklets

Preparation: Prepare one booklet for each student; the booklets will be kept and used for all eight weeks. Photocopy pages 37 and 38 back to back. Cut the pages on the dotted lines. Also cut blank sheets of paper in the same manner. Stack one blank half, one upper half and one lower half. Fold in the middle, with the blank sheet on the outside, and staple along the fold. Students can decorate and put their names on the front cover.

Instructions: Review the practice words for the day. Have the students pick a word from the first blend being covered (or you can pick for them) and think of all the words that be long in that word family and build them with the cubes. Example: If you are working with the "ai" combination, the students could make the following words: rain, brain, stain, plain and train. Have the students record their words in their booklets. Repeat this exercise for each blend covered that week.

Unit 2: Vowel Combinations

Activity 3: Create-a-Sentence

Materials: Unifix Blend Cubes
Unifix Consonant and Vowel Cubes
Pencil and Paper

Instructions: This activity is a follow-up from Activity 2, which uses word families. The objective is for students to use two words from the same family in the same sentence. First they select a word from the Practice Word list. They then think of a word that rhymes with the first word, and make up a sentence using both words. Have them write the sentence on their paper, leaving a blank for the Practice Word on their paper. Have the students build the Practice Word and place it in their sentence. Example: The _____ (train) is driving through the rain.

Activity 4: Word Webs

Materials: Word Web Worksheet, page 39

Instructions: This activity is geared for Weeks 1, 6 and 7. The word webs will be used to contrast vowel combinations that have the same sound, but are spelled differently. For example, you could use the vowel combination "oi" and "oy." Students write the letters "oi" in the top oval and the letters "oy" in the lower oval. Students then write words that use the vowel combinations on the lines that surround the ovals.

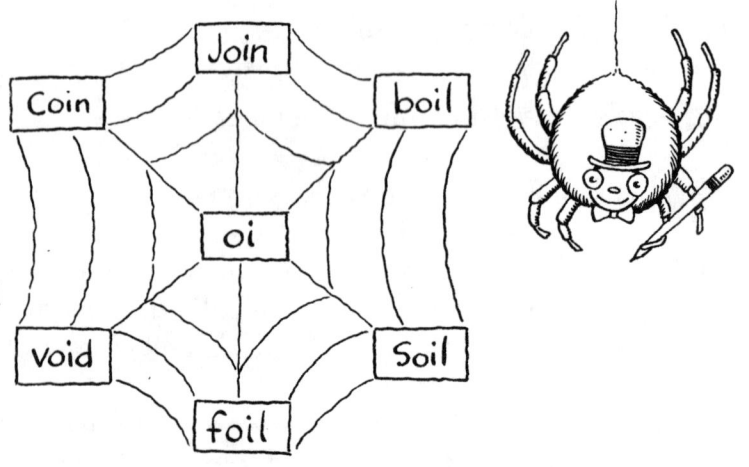

30   Unifix Phonics Blends

Activity 5: Alphabetizing Practice

Materials: Alphabetizing Practice Worksheet, page 25

Instructions: Pass out an Alphabetizing Practice Worksheet to each student. Have children alphabetize the words created in Activity 2.

Activity 6: Synonyms

Materials: Unifix Blend Cubes
Unifix Consonant and Vowel Cubes

Instructions: This activity has the students think about synonyms, which are words that have the same meanings. Select a word from the Practice Words and ask the students to build a synonym with their cubes. Example: If the word is hat, the students could build the word cap. See page 52 for more examples.

Unit 2: Vowel Combinations 31

Activity 7: Antonyms

Materials: Unifix Blend Cubes
Unifix Consonant and Vowel Cubes

Instructions: This activity has the students think about antonyms, which are words that have opposite meanings. Select a word from the Practice Words and ask the students to build an antonym with their cubes. Example: If the word is loud, the students would build the word quiet. See page 52 for more examples.

Activity 8: Homonyms

Materials: Unifix Blend Cubes
Unifix Consonant and Vowel Cubes

Instructions: This activity has the students think about homonyms, which are words that sound the same, but are spelled differently. Select a word from the Practice Words and ask the students to build a homonym with their cubes. Example: If the word is steel, the students would build the word steal. See page 52 for more examples.

32 Unifix Phonics Blends

Week 1 Vowel Combinations: ai, ay, ea, ee

These vowel combinations follow the rule that states: When two vowels go walking, the first one does the talking and the second one makes the first say its own name.

Practice Words:

ai	ay	ea	ee
brain	stray	each	teeth
trail	crayon	leaf	steel
stair	today	stream	free
grain	tray	please	street

Additional Words: _____ _____ _____ _____
_____ _____ _____ _____
_____ _____ _____ _____
_____ _____ _____ _____

Specific Activities: _____
_____
_____
_____

Week 2 Vowel Combinations: ie, oa, ue

These vowel combinations follow the rule that states: When two vowels go walking, the first one does the talking and the second one makes the first say its own name.

Practice Words:

ie	oa	ue
fried	float	blue
tries	cloak	clues
pie	toad	true
dries	roast	Tuesday

Additional Words: _____ _____ _____
_____ _____ _____
_____ _____ _____
_____ _____ _____

Specific Activities: _____
_____
_____
_____

Unit 2: Vowel Combinations   33

Week 3 Vowel Combinations: ar, er, ir

These vowel combinations can be taught together because they are r-controlled vowels.

Practice Words:

ar	er	ir
carpet	stern	dirt
star	dessert	skirt
starve	herd	stir
alarm	clerk	girl

Additional Words: _____ _____ _____
_____ _____ _____
_____ _____ _____
_____ _____ _____

Specific Activities: _____
_____
_____
_____

Week 4 Vowel Combinations: or, ur

These vowel combinations can be taught together because they are r-controlled vowels.

Practice Words:

or	ur
thorn	Thursday
orange	burn
color	hurt
horse	curly

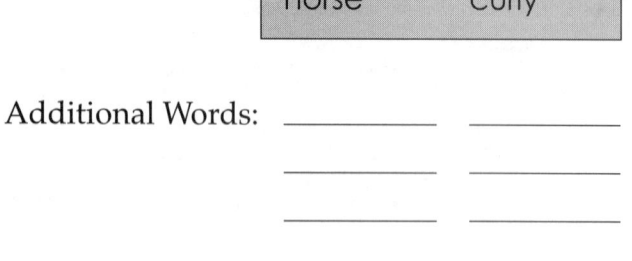

Additional Words: _____ _____
_____ _____
_____ _____
_____ _____

Specific Activities: _____
_____
_____
_____
_____

34 Unifix Phonics Blends

Week 5 Vowel Combinations: aw, ew

These vowel combinations can be taught together because they follow an _w pattern.

Practice Words:

aw	ew
straw	stew
flaw	blew
crawl	crew
dawn	jewel

Additional Words: _____ _____
_____ _____
_____ _____
_____ _____

Specific Activities: _____
_____
_____
_____

• •

Week 6 Vowel Combinations: oi, oy

These vowel combinations can be taught together because they have a similar sound.

Practice Words:

oi	oy
join	annoy
coin	ahoy
void	royal
spoil	enjoy

Additional Words: _____ _____
_____ _____
_____ _____
_____ _____

Specific Activities: _____
_____
_____
_____

Unit 2: Vowel Combinations

Week 7 Vowel Combinations: ou, ow

These vowel combinations can be taught together because they have a similar sound.

Practice Words:

ou	ow
snout	crown
clout	plow
grouch	fowl
mouth	shower

Additional Words: _____   _____
_____   _____
_____   _____
_____   _____

Specific Activities: _____
_____
_____
_____

Week 8 Vowel Combinations: ea, oo, ow

These are irregular vowel combinations.

Practice Words:

ea	oo	oo	ow
bread	took	spool	snow
health	book	spoon	below
ahead	crook	tooth	flown
treasure	look	smooth	owner

Additional Words: _____ _____ _____ _____
_____ _____ _____ _____
_____ _____ _____ _____
_____ _____ _____ _____

Specific Activities: _____
_____
_____
_____

36   Unifix Phonics Blends

•Week 8 Families•

ea	oo
1. _____	1. _____
2. _____	2. _____
3. _____	3. _____
4. _____	4. _____
5. _____	5. _____

oo	ow
1. _____	1. _____
2. _____	2. _____
3. _____	3. _____
4. _____	4. _____
5. _____	5. _____

•Week 1 Families•

ai	ay
1. _____	1. _____
2. _____	2. _____
3. _____	3. _____
4. _____	4. _____
5. _____	5. _____

ea	ee
1. _____	1. _____
2. _____	2. _____
3. _____	3. _____
4. _____	4. _____
5. _____	5. _____

•Week 6 Families•

oi	oy
1. _____	1. _____
2. _____	2. _____
3. _____	3. _____
4. _____	4. _____
5. _____	5. _____

•Week 3 Families•

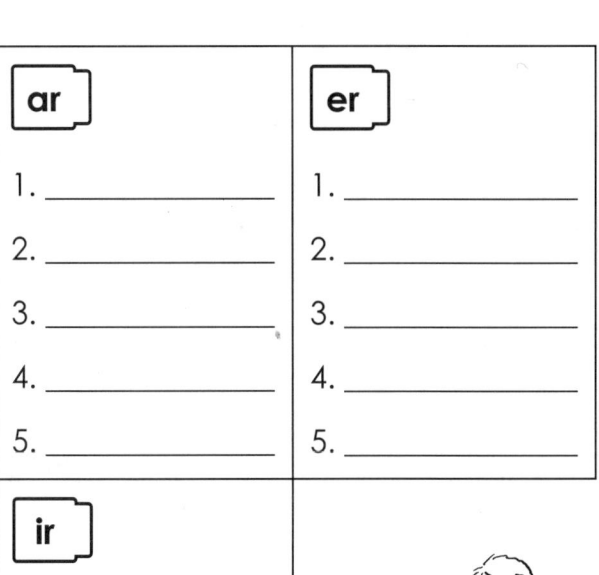

ar	er
1. _____	1. _____
2. _____	2. _____
3. _____	3. _____
4. _____	4. _____
5. _____	5. _____

ir
1. _____
2. _____
3. _____
4. _____
5. _____

•Week 2 Families•

ie	oa
1. _____	1. _____
2. _____	2. _____
3. _____	3. _____
4. _____	4. _____
5. _____	5. _____

ue
1. _____
2. _____
3. _____
4. _____
5. _____

•Week 7 Families•

ou	ow
1. _____	1. _____
2. _____	2. _____
3. _____	3. _____
4. _____	4. _____
5. _____	5. _____

•Week 4 Families•

or	ur
1. _____	1. _____
2. _____	2. _____
3. _____	3. _____
4. _____	4. _____
5. _____	5. _____

•Week 5 Families•

aw	ew
1. _____	1. _____
2. _____	2. _____
3. _____	3. _____
4. _____	4. _____
5. _____	5. _____

Name: _____

Word Webs

Unit 2: Vowel Combinations 39

Word Lists: Vowel Combinations

ai
aim
aid
ailment
ail
rain
train
wait
tail
chain
jail
mail
pain
sail
afraid
brain
claim
gain
main
obtain
paid
wait
plain
laid
faint
grain
rail

ay
always
mayor
crayon
maybe
haystack
payment
day
say
away
play
may
today
pay
gray
bay
stay
way

ea
eat
each
east
easy
eagle
eager
easel
eaten

eastern
ease
neat
read
least
beat
clean
deal
leaf
feast
peach
meat
weak
sea
tea
flea

ee
eel
eerie
sleep
green
keep
street
feet
wheel
feel
seem
teeth
sweet
see
three
tree
free
bee
degree

ie
spied
lied
tried
fried
tied
cried
die
lie

oa
oak
oat
oath
oatmeal
oaf
coat
soap
road

coast
load
toast
goat
goal
loan
float
loaf
groan
foam
roast
croak
soak
cloak
roach
boast
coal
toad
moan
throat
coach

ue
glue
hue
due
clue
true
flue
rue
sue

ar
are
arm
army
art
artist
arctic
article
arch
armor
ark
arbor
card
farm
hard
part
large
garden
start
dark
yard
party
car
far

bar
jar
tar
mar
par
scar

er
camera
allergy
bakery
liberty
battery
her
mother
over
other
were
better
sister
under
after
water
another
baker
wonder
ever
offer
river

ir
girl
first
third
shirt
dirt
skirt
affirm
circle
girth
birth
circus
thirty
shirk
firm
stirrup
fir
sir
stir
whir

or
or
order
ore
orbit

orchestra
ordinary
Oregon
organ
oral
orchard
short
horn
fork
forget
born
cord
score
form
before
horse
story
corner
store
north
force
for
more
nor

ur
urn
urban
urchin
urge
urgent
turn
burn
hurry
curl
purse
purple
hurt
turkey
curb
nurse
surface
further
purpose
burst
surf
turtle
fur
occur
spur

aw
awful
awkward
awning
awe

awl
awfully
lawn
drawn
lawyer
hawk
lawful
yawn
tawny
drawer
born
shawl
law
jaw
draw
straw
thaw
paw
claw
flaw
gnaw

ew
stew
strew
flew
grew
crew
brew
drew
dew
few
pew
view
new
knew

oi
oil
join
point
voice
coin
choice
noise
broil
spoil
avoid
poison
boil
turmoil
coil
moisture
exploit
doily
soil
rejoice

sirloin
toil
void
joint

oy
oyster
royal
voyage
loyal
boycott
annoying
employer
boyhood
joyous
disloyal
loyalty
enjoyment
joyful
boyish
toy
joy
enjoy
employ
destroy
coy
cowboy
annoy

ou
out
our
ounce
oust
ouch
outer
hour
sound
about
around
round
scout
amount
aloud
found
council
ground
loud
cloud
mountain
doubt
count

ow
down
town

brown
flower
crowd
crown
cowboy
power
vowel
downward
towel
powder
tower
chowder
shower
how
now
cow
plow
allow
somehow
eyebrow
bow
sow
endow
vow
prow
snowplow
owl

ea
head
heavy
ready
thread
steady
dead
breath
dear
ahead
breakfast
already
feather
death
measure
instead
leather
meadow
pleasant
spread
heading
sweat
treasure
weather
dread
pleasure
bread

oo
look
good
hook
afoot
hood
took
wood
rook
hoof
crook
foot
stood
soot
cookie
brook
wool
cook

oo
ooze
soon
school
room
food
smooth
pool
tooth
cool
goose
troop
foot
boot
tool
mood
roof
loose
noon
too
zoo
tattoo
shampoo

ow
owe
own
bowl
snowball
show
low
slow
snow
row
yellow
follow
hollow

Unit Three: Final Blends

Activity 1: Practice Word Practice

Materials: Unifix Blend Cubes
Unifix Consonant and Vowel Cubes

Instructions: Write the blend for the day in large letters where all students in the group can see it. Have students build the provided Practice Words one by one. Discuss pronunciations of the blend and the words. Post the provided Practice Words prominently in the classroom for referral all week with other activities.

Activity 2: New Word Challenge

Materials: Unifix Blend Cubes
Unifix Consonant and Vowel Cubes

Instructions: Write the blend for the day where all students in the group can see the word. Have the students find the lettered cubes for that blend. Have the students take turns building new words that end in that blend. Some of the words they come up with may be in the Practice Word list. Challenge them to come up with new and different words.

Unit 3: Final Blends 43

Activity 3: Build-A-Word

Materials: Unifix Blend Cubes
Unifix Consonant and Vowel Cubes

Instructions: Select a final blend, and have the students generate as many words as they can using that blend. Then, have each student build one of those words. Once the words are built, have the group alphabetize the words.

Activity 4: Cube Draw

Materials: Unifix Blend Cubes
Unifix Consonant and Vowel Cubes
Paper bags

Instructions: Have the students find the cube for the blend you are working on today. Have the students place the consonant and vowel cubes in the bag. Have students pull out letters one at a time until they can make a word using the final blend of the day.

44   Unifix Phonics Blends

Activity 5: Word Unscramble

Materials: Unifix Blend Cubes
Unifix Consonant and Vowel Cubes

Instructions: Build a word from the Practice Words. Then, break the cubes apart and scramble the cubes. Have students take turns putting the cubes in the correct order.

Activity 6: Crossword Puzzle

Materials: Unifix Blend Cubes
Unifix Consonant and Vowel Cubes

Instructions: Have the students build each of the Practice Words with their cubes, without locking the cubes together. Ask them if they can arrange the words to form a crossword puzzle.

Unit 3: Final Blends

Activity 7: Build the Answer

Materials: Unifix Blend Cubes
Unifix Consonant and Vowel Cubes

Instructions: Recite a clue sentence to the students using a word from the Practice Words. Ask the students to find the Practice Word that completes the sentence, then build it with their cubes. Example: If a Practice Word is dream, you could tell the students this sentence, "You do this when you sleep." The students would build the word dream.

Activity 8: Partner Pass

Materials: Unifix Blend Cubes
Unifix Consonant and Vowel Cubes

Instructions: Divide the group into partners. Review the Practice Words. One student picks a word, and joins the first 2 or 3 letter cubes. Then he or she passes the cubes to his or her partner and lets them figure out which word has been started. The partner finishes building the word. Students take turns starting words.

46 Unifix Phonics Blends

Week 1 Final Blends: ch, ck, sh, th

These final blends can be taught together because they have two consonants that combine to make one sound.

Practice Words:

ch	ck	sh	th
beach	brick	flash	cloth
lunch	truck	bush	booth
touch	clock	swish	north
rich	thick	slosh	truth

Additional Words: _____ _____ _____ _____

Specific Activities: _____

Week 2 Final Blends: sk, ss, st

These final blends can be taught together because they have two consonants that make individual sounds.

Practice Words:

sk	ss	st
brisk	glass	test
flask	guess	forest
whisk	dress	chest
tusk	across	coast

Additional Words: _____ _____ _____

Specific Activities: _____

Unit 3: Final Blends 47

Week 3 Final Blends: nd, nt, lk, ll, lt

These final blends can be taught together because they both follow an **l_** pattern.

Practice Words:

ld	lf	lk	ll	lt
field	shelf	silk	stroll	adult
mold	gulf	milk	thrill	fault
behold	wolf		smell	melt
unfold	calf		quill	colt

Additional Words: _____ _____ _____ _____ _____

Specific Activities: _____

Week 4 Final Blends: ff, ft

These final blends can be taught together because they both follow an **f_** pattern.

Practice Words:

ff	ft
scuff	left
stiff	cleft
bluff	draft
sniff	soft

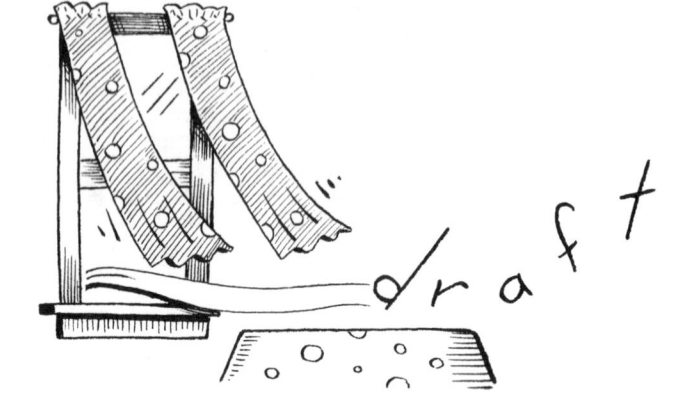

draft

Additional Words: _____ _____

Specific Activities: _____

48 Unifix Phonics Blends

Week 5 Final Blends: nd, nt

These final blends can be taught together because they both follow an **n**_ pattern.

Practice Words:

nd	nt
ground	plant
grind	front
behind	spent
fond	point

Additional Words: _____ _____
_____ _____
_____ _____
_____ _____

Specific Activities: _____
_____
_____
_____

• •

Week 6 Final Blends: mp

Practice Words:

mp
stomp
cramp
limp
swamp

Additional Words: _____
_____
_____
_____

Specific Activities: _____
_____
_____
_____

Unit 3: Final Blends   49

Week 7 Final Blends: ng, nk

These final blends can be taught together because they both follow an n_ pattern.

Practice Words:

ng	nk
sprang	blink
string	trunk
wrong	honk
belong	tank

Additional Words: _____ _____
_____ _____
_____ _____
_____

Specific Activities: _____
_____
_____
_____

Week 8 Final Blends: gh, gn, lk

These final blends can be taught together because they contain silent letters.

Practice Words:

gh	gn	lk
sigh	sign	yolk
high	resign	walk
bough	align	folk
dough	design	talk

Additional Words: _____ _____ _____
_____ _____ _____
_____ _____ _____
_____ _____ _____

Specific Activities: _____
_____
_____
_____

50   Unifix Phonics Blends

Word Lists: Final Blends

ch
which
each
much
such
beach
lunch
teach
rich
catch
branch
touch
inch
reach
watch

ck
clock
sock
mock
lock
flock
smock
trunk
thick
block
brick
stick
puck
pack
pick
pluck
muck
stuck

sh
wish
wash
fish
push
finish
flash
swish
slosh
fresh
rush
dish
crash
bush
flash
establish

th
with
both
booth
north
ninth
worth
cloth
teeth
truth
death
south
fifth
bath

sk
desk
task
ask
brisk
flask
whish
tusk
mask
husk
dusk

ss
dress
mess
glass
floss
bass
boss
truss
press
guess
across
moss
toss
bless
less
stress
caress
gloss
miss
hiss
mass
loss
bliss

st
best
cast
test
forest
chest
coast
dust
fast

least
past
west

ld
gold
could
would
should
behold
unfold
mold
sold
hold
told
cold
bold
fold
wild
mild
child
field
meld

lf
elf
shelf
golf
wolf
gulf
engulf
calf
half

lk
milk
elk
bilk
bulk
hulk
silk

ll
smell
tell
tall
ball
hall
mall
pill
swill
hill
thrill
quill
scroll
hull

doll
toll
stroll
stall
full
gull
small

lt
molt
adult
fault
melt
colt
bolt
dolt
hilt
stilt
malt
halt
fault
wilt
tilt
kilt
jilt
silt
salt
pelt
belt
felt

ff
stiff
sniff
scuff
off
scoff
muff
huff
bluff
buff
cuff
stuff
fluff
staff
miff
tiff
whiff

ft
aft
raft
daft
cleft
draft
craft

oft
soft
loft
shaft
left
sift
lift
rift

nd
hand
and
band
stand
bend
bond
bind
wind
wand
fond
ground
grind
behind
sand
send
tend
rend
trend
fend
rind
find
hind
pond
mend
mind
lend
land

nt
bent
sent
went
pant
front
spent
point
tent
tint
ant
lint
bunt
blunt
hunt
count
mount
dent

font
haunt
hint
jaunt
mint
pint
pant
punt
rent
stint
stunt

mp
lamp
camp
damp
ramp
tamp
stamp
stomp
swamp
romp
cramp
crimp
limp
blimp
rump
lump
bump
dump
hump
stump
jump
pump

ng
sing
bring
thing
going
swing
string
sprang
long
song
gang
hang
young
bang
lung
wing
ring
fling
spring
strong
fang

hung
string
wrong
belong

nk
ink
blink
stink
sink
mink
brink
tank
bank
sank
dank
yank
crank
monk
spunk
link
honk
hunk
chink
chunk
junk
funk
trunk
sunk

gh
high
sigh
through
weigh
though
sleigh
although
dough
neigh

gn
sign
benign
feign
campaign
resign
design
align

lk
folk
talk
walk
stalk
yolk

Unit 3: Final Blends 51

Appendix A: Synonym/Antonym/Homonym Word Lists

Synonyms

trail .... path
stair .... step
stream .... creek
street............. road
cloak .... cape
clue .... hint
carpet .... rug
dirt................ mud

stir .... mix
hurt............... pain
jewel .... gem
enjoy .... like
fowl .... bird
look .... see
smooth .... soft
below .... under

Antonyms

stray .... near
free .... caged
fried .... raw
float .... sink
true .... false
starve .... feed
curly .... straight

stearn .... kind
join................ separate
enjoy .... dislike
grouch .... happy
health .... sickness
ahead .... behind
took .... gave

Homonyms

ai
stair .... stare
plain .... plane
pair .... pare, pear
wait .... weight
maid .... made
tail................ tale
mail .... male

ea
heard .... herd
break .... brake

ou
foul .... fowl

ue
blue .... blew

ee
steel .... steal
meet .... meat
see................ sea
feet............... feat

oa
road .... rode
board .... bored
toad .... towed

ie
tied .... tide

52 Unifix Phonics Blends

Appendix B: Blend Clip Art

This clip art covers many of the blends in this book. You can make copies, enlarge, color the pictures, or scan them into your computer. Uses include:

- Making flashcards
- Creating game cards
- Enlarging and coloring to make mini posters
- Assembling into mini books

chair	chicken	ship	shell	think
thorn	wheel	whale	broom	brick
crab	crown	dress	drum	frog
friends	grass	grapes	present	price
tree	trumpet	blanket	bloom	clock

Appendix B 53

Blend Clip Art

clown	fly	flag	globe	glass
slide	slippers	scarf	scooter	skunk
skate	smell	smile	snail	snake
spider	space	star	stamp	swan
sweep	twins	twelve	train	nail
hay	leaf	read	sheep	feet

Blend Clip Art

shield	coat	soap	glue	statue
car	bark	mermaid	fern	bird
skirt	fork	corn	turtle	purse
draw	strawberry	jewel	blew	oil
coins	oyster	boy	mouse	house
cow	flower	bread	feather	book

Appendix B 55

Blend Clip Art

wood	moon	spoon	burrow	shadow
lunch	branch	duck	sack	fish
dish	bath	mouth	desk	tusk
ghost	nest	tent	ant	ball
doll	raft	pond	hand	lump
lamp	king	string	drink	ink

56 Unifix Phonics Blends Appendix B **56**